# GARDENING FOR THE SOUL

## Cultivating the Life God Wants You to Live

David L. Mahan

ISBN 979-8-89130-543-4 (paperback)
ISBN 979-8-89130-544-1 (digital)



Christian Faith Publishing
832 Park Avenue
Meadville, PA 16335
www.christianfaithpublishing.com

Printed in the United States of America

To my wonderful grandmother,
Joanna Magdalene Mahan
A truly loving *gardener of souls*—mine included

It is my heartfelt intent in writing this book to share lessons learned through my own mistakes, regrets, loss, and joyful victories over nearly sixty years of living, mostly walking with the Lord. In no way is the intent to pass judgment or even criticism but rather to offer humble suggestions for prayerful consideration and self-examination.

To provide advance clarification, the words *heart* and *soul* shall be used throughout this book in a somewhat interchangeable and synonymous manner. The debate over the soul being more the mind, will, and emotions, while the heart typically refers more to a person's spirit, can wait for another time and place.

Please enjoy these helpful gardening tips.

# CHAPTER 1

# Fallow Ground

If a person desires a beautiful garden full of vibrant flowers with brilliant colors or healthy crops rich in nutrients, they must first have fertile soil. No one in their right mind would ever waste good seed haphazardly tossed onto dry, crusty soil full of rocks and weeds. To expect any fruitful harvest from that kind of planting would be ludicrous. That is the futility of what Matthew 13 warns us about with Jesus's parable:

> The farmer went out to sow his seed. As he was scattering the seed, some fell along the path, and the birds came and ate it up. Some fell on rocky places, where it did not have much soil. It sprang up quickly because the

soil was shallow. But when the sun came up, the plants were scorched, and they withered because they had no root. Other seed fell among thorns, which grew up and choked the plants.

Then Jesus goes on to encourage us, "Still other seed fell on good soil, where it produced a crop—a hundred, sixty, or thirty times what was sown."

So it is with our own soul. If one desires to yield a fruitful spiritual life, they must begin with examining the soil of their heart. In Ezekiel 36:26, God promises those who are willing and obedient, "I will give you a new heart and put a new spirit in you; I will remove from you your heart of stone and give you a heart of flesh." What a beautiful and hopeful assurance that our Heavenly Father can and will give us a heart and soul that is tender and open to receiving the seed of His Word and Spirit. To remove what is dead and so dry that it has become lifeless as a rock, and then replace it with a life-giving, life-producing vessel through which His anointing and blessing can flow freely. This, in turn, is what gives the individual the privilege and honor of planting other seeds in the lives within their sphere of influence. Just as a healthy wildflower disseminates its seed as the wind carries it, so also the Spirit of God takes the words of life that we speak if we are willing and surrendered to whomever He chooses.

Yet this miraculous occurrence cannot take place unless the soul is fertile enough to receive the Seed that God wishes to impregnate in our lives first. Just as it says in Hosea 10:12 (NIV), "Sow righteousness for yourselves, reap the fruit of unfailing love, and break up your fallow ground; for it is time to seek the LORD, until He comes and showers His righteousness on you."

It is only by seeking the LORD in continuous, sincere prayer and worship that we will see the fallow ground in our lives—the roots of bitterness, pride, envy, and malice—broken up and removed. Then and only then can we truly receive that which God wants to impart in us and through us.

But how does our soul's "soil" become fallowed? I believe it is a very pernicious work of the enemy, Satan. It usually occurs over time, not all at once, lest we might recognize it more easily. There are many root causes, such as unforgiveness, hatred, pride, or even the more subtle, jealousy and envy. Pride, which is, in this author's opinion, the original sin, can produce an extremely hardened and unfruitful soil. The reason I hold this opinion is that the Bible tells us that was the reason for Satan's fall and subsequently being cast out of heaven. James 4:6 says, "God opposes the proud but shows favor to the humble." We never want to be in a place where God is opposing us, but rather, humble yourself, and God promises to lift you up (1 Peter 5:6 and James 4:10).

The main reason pride is an exceptionally common cause of fallow ground is due to its inherent trademark of not being receptive to any form of instruction or correction. Therefore, the only real way to counteract the residue of pride is to humble ourselves on a daily basis. It is not sufficient to merely pray the prayer once, "LORD, teach me humility. Help me walk in humility as Christ did." We must be sedulous to pray that vulnerable and sincere prayer every day since the sin of pride is so ubiquitous in our society and in the "human condition." As we open ourselves up to the humbling and sanctifying work of the Holy Spirit, we can begin to see the "unholy roots" in our heart's soil disappear. Always remember, it is better to humble ourselves first because if God has to humble us, it's usually too late then—the damage is already done.

Unforgiveness and bitterness are probably the next most frequent reasons for a person's heart to be full of unhealthy soil—fallow ground. The main reason here is due to the callousness produced within our heart from harboring offenses instead of letting go through love and understanding. I realize this is much easier said than done, especially when considering some of the egregious and even malicious acts that are committed sometimes, even within families. Yet we must recognize that to not forgive means we're giving the other person or the offense control over our lives. Not to mention the cancerous effect bitterness and unforgiveness can have on our health, both physical and mental.

Plus, all too often, we fail to remember the sobering words of Jesus in Matthew 6:15, "But if you do not forgive others their trespasses, your Father will not forgive your trespasses." This is most definitely not a nugatory suggestion but rather a daunting admonition and command, with severe consequences if unheeded. We should always attempt to put ourselves in the other person's place and try to understand where the offensive statement or action is really coming from. Most often, offenses are either the result of the person's own pain, insecurity, and past issues unresolved, or a misunderstanding maybe, or perhaps a rigid expectation that wasn't fair or reasonable to begin with. I once heard someone refer to the "unholy trinity" as meaning the following—judgments, comparisons, and rigid expectations.

First, we have to understand that none of us were ever meant to be the judge of anyone. Prior to the fall in the Garden of Eden, man and woman were to avoid eating from the Tree of the Knowledge of Good and Evil. God knew then that mankind was not capable of receiving or processing that kind of information without it tarnishing our outlook and opinion of one another. He wanted His creation to maintain a certain childlike innocence and view on life, hence only eating from the Tree of Life. Ever notice how a child never seems to hold a grudge or offense toward someone for very long, if at all? They are always quick to forgive, even faster to forget, and most certainly open to accepting others with unconditional love.

Next, comparing oneself to another is a very slippery slope. It always leads to lack of satisfaction and contentment. In a perpetuating cycle, we find ourselves chasing just one more—one more achievement, one more accolade, or one more change.

The lust of the eyes and lust of the flesh in the end leave behind a cement-like layer over our soul that prevents real joy and peace from permeating into our lives. If only we could see how each of us is a unique creation fearfully and wonderfully made by the Master's hand with special gifts and talents for a specific reason and purpose. Instead, we waste our time and energy climbing over that next hill only to find the grass isn't any greener at all. In fact, sometimes it's dead, as is now also what we left behind. The marriage we thought could be replaced, the career we failed to see was really our true calling all along; or the home we never realized was actually heaven lying at our feet.

Then there are rigid expectations. Expectations, to a certain extent, are not dangerous or wrong, necessarily. But when they become the master—controlling our thoughts, reactions, and motives—then they can become the worst kind of topsoil in our hearts. Topsoil that is full of thorns that hurt those around us. Thorns that end up keeping those we love at arm's length, precluding real intimacy and love. I believe this is the toughest to cure of all the culprits for fallow ground. This is where the "plow" by itself isn't enough. We must first water the hardened ground with accountability and saturating prayer. Proverbs 27:17 (NIV) says, "As iron sharpens iron, so one person sharpens another." I love one translation that says, "And a man sharpens the face of a friend" (LSV).

That's an incredible picture of what accountability within a committed friendship or marriage is to look like. Just as the plow a farmer uses to break up that fallow ground won't be as effective unless it has been first sharpened, so it is also with our words. Since the power of life and death is in the spoken word, as the Bible tells us, we should always be asking the Holy Spirit to speak through us with His life-giving, transformative words that will cut through the hardened topsoil of defensive attitudes, shame, or fear and expose what lies beneath. Hebrews 4:12 (NIV) tells us, "For the Word of God is living and active. Sharper than any double-edged sword, it penetrates even to dividing soul and spirit, joints and marrow; it judges the thoughts and attitudes of the heart."

Lastly, grief is also a common precipitating event which can lead to fallow ground in our heart and soul. Certainly, it is understandable and not an easy one to fix either. I say this with the utmost compassion since I know all too well of what I speak. In my midtwenties, both my parents were killed in a car accident. It was a tragedy which left my life in an unraveling state for several years. Besides the failure of my marriage at that time, which was certainly collateral damage, there were other unintended consequences incurred—a hardened heart among the worst. I blamed God at first. And although I turned to Him ultimately in prayer and worship for inner healing and direction, still I didn't realize until years later the toxic fallout that remained in my soul. This fallout I speak of was a residue manifested in rigid expectations that would, and still does, haunt me to this day.

Since my parents' death was so very shocking and unpredictable, I began to insist that everything else in my life must be inveterate and always go according to plan. There was no room for change, spontaneity, or capricious outcomes. At least now I am aware of this dire need to continually surrender this "thorn" to the LORD since He has already borne all our thorns in the crown of scorn He wore on the Cross. And then asking those closest to me for prayerful support and accountability has helped immensely. While the grief journey I walked through, very slowly at times, did eventually wane and acceptance came, I have become exceedingly aware of the absolute importance of life-affirming relationships within the blessing of family and community. This brings healing and sanctifying renewal. Then we find the fertile soil rich in nutrients and, in turn, can receive the seed of truth that sets us free.

# CHAPTER 2

# Weeds of Iniquity

So you've done the labor-intensive work of breaking up that fallow ground, and now you are enjoying rich, fertile soil ready for sowing seeds of life. However, you continue to see these persisting and menacing weeds in your life. These weeds are actually recurring struggles with sins and bad habits you thought were long since confessed and repented of. This condition is what Scripture refers to as iniquity. Iniquity is the residue from sin. It is the underlying proclivity to repeat an act or attitude that you know is in fact harmful for you, yet you can't seem to bring under full control. This is the phenomenon that the Apostle Paul referred to in Romans chapter 7. He said, "That which I want to do I don't; yet that which I don't want to do, that is what I do." Paul understood there are things from our past, which are like hooks or strongholds that the enemy has established. And only God, in His infinite power and authority, can remove and destroy them.

I remember going fishing for the first time as a young boy. When I caught my first fish, I was so excited and proud I couldn't wait to take it home and have my mom cook it for supper. There were just two minor details standing in my way. First, there was this hook I had to remove. Now, as I began to fumble around with it, I realized it was in there pretty good, deeply embedded and most assuredly not going to come out easily. After about ten minutes of failed attempts to coax it out, in my youthful exuberance I just ripped it out—along with part of the fish's mouth. Of course, the fish was already dead, but the trophy I would later present to my hungry family was certainly diminished. At that point, I realized it would have been best to invoke the assistance of my father, who was having no trouble whatsoever in removing his hooks from the plethora of fish he had caught.

So it is with these persistent hooks embedded in the fabric of our soul, there is only One truly qualified to remove them; the Holy Spirit with His faithful, sanctifying work. Now because God is a gentleman and will not impose Himself on anyone, we must, upon recognizing the need exists, ask our Heavenly Father for divine assistance. Just as my father that day on the lake shore was not going to deprive me of the chance to remove the hook myself, so also our Heavenly Father will graciously wait for our plea for help. It takes longer sometimes for certain hooks to be removed depending on how deep they are or how entangled they might be with other commingling spiritual tissue, such as "soul ties" from past relationships or word curses spoken over us. But once the hook is successfully removed, it is imperative we allow the Holy Spirit to heal and fill that area in our heart with His sanctifying presence.

This is the second step I referred to earlier that had to occur after the hook was removed from the fish's mutilated mouth. It had to be cleaned before the trophy could be enjoyed. This cleaning process is not always fun, and for a young boy, it was certainly messy. However, it was essential, for without the cleaning, the fish would never have become life-giving nourishment to my family. So it is with the cleaning God wants to do in our heart and soul, removing that which is now dead and spoiling and replacing it with carefully prepared spiritual nourishment from His Word. We must soak in God's presence by letting His Word become inculcated in our lives. As we feed on the Holy Scriptures, we will receive insight and direction on how to tear down the strongholds that have kept us from enjoying life abundantly! Just remember, when those strongholds are vanquished from our lives, the space they used to occupy must be filled with something healthy and holy. Otherwise, we can create a spiritual vacuum, unintentionally, that could become inhabited by an even worse carnal, selfish desire or habit.

These strongholds are serious business and should never be treated insouciantly. In fact, it's wise to consult your pastor, spiritual mentor, or Christian counselor for guidance on how to pray specifically regarding this serious matter, as well as other ameliorating actions needed. Don't misunderstand, the eventual demise of the stronghold has already been accomplished through the precious blood of Christ on the Cross, and because of an empty tomb. However, there are subtle layers of unholy agreements we make sometimes unknowingly that are the impetus to a stronghold being established. These agreements, or soul ties as they are also called, must be identified, repealed, and obliterated first before the "strongman" can be evicted from our soul. Deliverance ministry is something always requiring prayerful, loving, and compassionate support.

Pruning is an essential part of this also. By this I mean the willingness to get rid of habits, predilections, or even certain relationships that can give way to temptation, sin, or counterproductive strife. I once heard a pastor share a tragicomic story about a man who had struggled with pornography for years. He told his pastor one day how he wanted more than anything to be free from this destructive habit. He had tried every seminar and read every book he could find, yet to no avail, he still struggled. Then, shockingly, he mentioned how every time he would walk past that adult bookstore on the way to work, he felt such incredible temptation. The pastor, upon hearing this, immediately offered the suggestion, "Take a different route to work!" Just as with pruning a rose bush, the key is to identify what is dead or dying and remove it—that which could contaminate other areas of our life if left unattended.

Another example: if every time you talk with someone, the conversation ends up being a stressful diatribe, perhaps that is a relationship you should walk away from. Still love that person, of course, but if all they do is irritate you and promote animosity, then it's far better to eliminate the risk to save your heart—and theirs. The Bible teaches us to love one another; that doesn't mean we have to like everyone. Now, if there is something that needs to be said or done to heal and rectify an offense made, then by all means take that step and make the effort for reconciliation before giving up.

While there are certainly some steps that are quite arduous, we must take to see real breakthrough, there are also some relatively simple and easy preventive measures we can implement right away. Again, as with pruning a rose bush, it promotes healthy future growth, albeit hard to see initially with the plant looking bare; removing the dead portions is a necessity to make room for new life. Our souls can get so full of unhealthy influences, relationships, habits. This is where prayerful discernment and accountability from your closest friends and family will help sort out what should stay and what we should get rid of. Don't be reluctant to ask for this input. It is hard sometimes to see the truth for ourselves; having a trusted confidant with a more objective vantage point can make all the difference between growth and stagnation.

The question facing each of us from the LORD—how much do we want healing, transformation, and freedom? It is crucial to remember what we don't deal with in our lives now could very well be passed down to the next generation. For just as there are generational blessings, there are certainly also generational curses.

## Children of Shame

Something there is that owns a child, that trades their
    pride for false guilt.
And perhaps for life remain beguiled, with fear mis-
    placed and often built.
Their hearts lay burdened with no just plea, trans-
    gressions are another thing.
For that is guilt owned honestly, redemption paid for
    everything.


Yet tormented souls, morose and driven, their
    strength is spent on vain remorse.
And futile search for selves forgiven, martyrs by
    name, though children of course.
They sing their anthem loud and clear:
"I shall accept the blame for naught."
Though naught begot naught, and shame begets fear.
And children make poor scapegoats.

Their forebearers denied and refused to accept,
Their guilt and consequence.
Unwilling to own their err or sin,
Thus, offspring now to recompense.


For she is love unfaithful, and I am man once killed.
Each hidden stain and blemish truthful, a hallowed
	secret never willed.
Hence image saved and cherished dear, though casu-
	alties surrender self.
Fettered by chains of shame and fear, for acceptance
	now deny thyself.
Yes, children make poor scapegoats.


Unaware of ghost in closet hid, 'til time when all shall
	be revealed.
Then learn they must all shame to rid, with guilt
	returned—esteem thus sealed,
For children make poor scapegoats.

# CHAPTER 3

# Seeds of Praise and Gratitude

The most productive way to plant a new garden is to visualize what you want it to look like when it's all grown in. To envision the end result with joyful anticipation helps make the routine of planting and nurturing delightful and successful. This, of course, applies to the human soul as well. When we start to plant healthy seeds in our life, seeds of praise and thanksgiving unto the One who has given us life are incomparably paramount. Scripture tells us in Psalm 103:1–5,

> Praise the Lord, my soul; all my inmost being, praise His holy name. Praise the Lord, my soul and forget not all His benefits—who forgives all your sins

and heals all your diseases, who
redeems your life from the pit
and crowns you with love and
compassion, who satisfies your
desires with good things so that
your youth is renewed like the
eagle's.

We always have something to thank God for,
even if we can't seem to get past the moment of stress,
failure, or temptation.

Praising God in the midst of the storm is the
fastest way to see breakthrough – to see our outlook
improve. Again, I realize this is easier said than done,
especially when we may have just experienced the loss
of a loved one, some negative medical report, or perhaps rejection by a trusted friend. Still, these are the
times that we will look back on throughout eternity
as "going from victory to victory" if only we can see
past the temporal into the eternal with Heaven's eyes.
There has been nothing in my life that has brought
me into God's presence quicker than praising Him.
Certainly, it's easy when the news is good, the disease is gone, the prodigal child has returned, or the
long-awaited promotion has happened. And most
definitely, those are the times we must stop to give
thanks and praise to whom it is due—the Almighty
Creator. However, at times when pain, grief, fear, and
doubt come to visit us as an unwelcome guest, with
an overwhelming shadow of despair, that is the most
critical moment to take our eyes off the albeit seri-

ous adversity and fix our gaze on God and His sovereignty. There alone will we find the strength to meet those challenges with resolve and unyielding courage.

The Bible is replete with examples of praise being used as a weapon for battle. The walls of Jericho came tumbling down due to God's people praising with shouts and ram's horns (instruments of worship). Jail cell doors suddenly were opened for Paul and Silas due to their praise and worship of the Almighty. David facing Goliath in battle was prefaced with praise and recognition of who God is and that "the battle is the LORD's." There is great power released when we acknowledge God for who He is and what He has done. Even declaring and praising God for what is yet to come is a strategy for success in the battlefield of our souls. In 2 Corinthians 10:5, the Bible instructs us to "take every thought captive and make it obedient to Christ." The concept here of taking captive implies a battle is underway. And as in every battle, there is victory and defeat. Jesus Christ, the Risen One, has already won the battle for us—the victory is His! Therefore, taking those thoughts and ideas captive immediately is imperative before they can influence our lives in a way that leads to destruction and death.

In Joshua chapter 7 verse 19, we are told, "Then Joshua said to Achan, 'My son, give glory to the Lord, the God of Israel, and honor Him. Tell me what you have done; do not hide it from me.'" I have always found it interesting that Joshua didn't start off by rebuking Achan or threatening to punish him for his sin, although in the end he still was punished. Rather, the very first thing Joshua tells Achan to do is give glory and honor to God. Unfortunately, that was not Achan's response. I've often wondered if the outcome might have been different had Achan immediately started by falling prostrate, giving praise and worship to the Most High God. Certainly, there still would have been consequences for the broken covenant. However, perhaps Achan's entire family would have been spared. The point being that praise unto God is always the best place to start in every situation. We never know until later how that simple yet profoundly humble act can alter the outcome. One thing for certain, starting from a posture of praise and worship will always lead to greater surrender and obedience.

Planting seeds of praise always ushers us into a place of focusing on the things of God instead of the things of this world. This posture can provide us with greater insight and discernment into what the proper response should be to whatever the conundrum is we're wrestling with at the time. Praise and worship clear our mind and heart of things that are clouding our judgment and preventing us from hearing God's voice. These things may, in fact, be normal, innocuous things—such as how to balance our budget that's in the red, how to motivate our kids to try harder in school, or maybe how to tell our spouse we don't appreciate the way they're treating us. Yet again they may be persistent temptations or recurring fears we can't seem to overcome. Either way, whatever the source of the distraction, nothing will provide greater clarity and perception than entering into God's "gates with thanksgiving and His courts with praise." Once we're in that secret place and the LORD is inhabiting our praises, as His Word promises He will, we can find true rest and peace for our weary souls.

Lastly, praise and worship are the one sure way to humble ourselves and recognize that God is the center of the universe—and not us. Even "praising" and honoring others for their noble attributes is a great way to remind oneself of our own imperfection and humanity. I once heard a pastor liken the ones we love, such as our spouse or children, to a beautiful garden. He said if we don't tend to that garden with a loving and deliberately careful approach, then that garden could become sick (heartsick) and lose its beauty and joy-evoking presence. The best way to cultivate and maintain the beautiful "gardens" in our lives that God has entrusted us with is by paying tribute to and honoring them with both words and acts of love and recognition.

Affirming our loved ones daily will build up their sense of worth and value like nothing else can. After all, we are called to be our Savior's hands and mouth, speaking His words of life and love. We must always be cognizant of what's dying around us. To discern what's being choked out by thorns of bitterness or neglect, what is in dire need of water and nourishment, and what is lacking in the sunshine of our own presence and attention. Speak words of praise, gratitude, and affection, first and foremost to our God; and then, in turn, with God's love exuding from our hearts, speak words of praise, gratitude, and affection to the ones whom God places in our journey.

# CHAPTER 4

# Fertilizing with Friendship

I realize this is a somewhat peculiar and amusing title for a chapter, and certainly, we have all had friends that might have been a little "crappy" at times. However, that's not what this chapter is about. Rather, it's an encouragement to each of us to be the type of friend to others that provides proper life-giving nourishment to their souls. No one knows you like your best friend, spouse, or maybe your siblings. Regardless of the role, it's those closest to you who should know what makes you tick, and what brings you out of those darkest moments back into God's glorious light. If you have been entrusted with that kind of information about someone else, then how are you using it? Are you using that intel to build that friend up with encouragement when they're down and out? Or are you using it as a manipulative tool to get what you want out of the relationship? The *golden rule* is a timeless guide on how to live our lives: "Do unto others as you would have them do unto you."

One of the main reasons I always admired my father's side of our family is consistency. I have many cousins and other relatives that have lived in the same town their entire life. While it's not an absolute prerequisite to establishing great friends, it does certainly help when we stick around somewhere for a long period of time. I recently moved back to Arizona, where I grew up, after being away for thirty years. Besides being totally shocked by the unprecedented growth the metro Phoenix area has seen in the last three decades, I was also shocked to learn how many of my childhood friends were gone. They had moved away, as did I, although I just assumed they would always be there—frozen in time. The friends that were still there, much to my surprise and disappointment, didn't seem to have much in common with me anymore. No one's fault, just the result of growing older apart from one another for that long a period. How I wish the immortal words of Thomas Wolfe, "You can't go home again," weren't so true and relevant.

My reason for mentioning this was not just to lament and wax nostalgically but rather to emphasize how important it is to seize the day. No one knows what the future holds except the One who holds the future in His hand. Therefore, since we have no guarantee we'll be here tomorrow, let's make the most of each day we're blessed with and be a blessing to those

God has entrusted within our care—our friends and family. One way to do this is simply to demonstrate how much we value their presence in our lives and show them we are honored to know who they truly are. To be known is one of life's greatest gifts. We should treasure that and, in turn, treasure those within our God-given sphere of influence. Now, it's not always peaches and cream with words of heartwarming affection. Sometimes it's tough love that is required. If a friend is truly a trusted confidant, then they should know when the appropriate time is for correction and constructive criticism. As mentioned earlier in this book, Proverbs 27:17 says, "As iron sharpens iron, so one person sharpens another." And Proverbs 27:6 reminds us, "Faithful are the wounds of a friend." Just be sure to have the disinfectant and bandages of love and compassion handy after the wound has been delivered. That way, healing and growth can be accomplished in that friend's life, not just the correction. This is why accountability is such an essential part of friendship.

I have been so richly blessed in my life with two sisters, a son, and my lovely wife, who are all such amazing supporters and encouragers of me. I am never at a loss for affirmation or unconditional love. That's not to say there hasn't been times when I was in the wrong and had for some reason made a bad decision that they knew needed to be addressed. Yet it was always within the confines of their best interest in my ultimate good and betterment that the confrontation took place. I have always greatly appreciated their faithful advice, admonishment, and affirmation.

In the end, as the old saying goes, you only take with you the relationships out of this world. The big bank account, the nice house, the fancy car, and the trophies are all going to fade away someday. But relationships, friendships, that's what will be waiting for us on the other side of glory. I never want to get to heaven only to find out I could have done more to assure my loved ones that they were truly loved and treasured by me. Now is the time for us all to pour into each other's lives with the fertilizing nourishment of friendship. Tomorrow is not promised. The question we should ask ourselves, which is so very telling, is, "What do you want said about yourself at your funeral?"

> Where did I go that day to die?
> In meadow green or ocean deep;
> And at the end of suffering's cry,
> Did I my soul then pray to keep?
> Or did I leave this earthly place,
> With heartbeat fast, for fear to rid.
> And head hung low in deep disgrace;
> For coward in some cavern hid?
> Was it with friendship rich in love,
> That I departed temporal plane?
> Or was it with no thought above,
> Empty, alone and with disdain?
> And was the place where I last fell,
> Turned into shrine or sacred ground?

Or was it feared and shame to tell,
If ever there you could be found?
I hope it was in battle fierce,
That I laid down my soul to rest.
With cold steel sword through heart did pierce,
To grant me die of courage—best.
Where did I go to die that day?
When reaper came with sickle raised.
A place of pride and honor pray;
Where men who went before were praised.

# Watering with the Word

Psalm 63 says, "God, you are my God, earnestly I seek you; my soul thirsts for you, my body longs for you, in a dry and weary land where there is no water."

There is no way to sustain life without water, just as there's no way to sustain and grow a healthy spiritual life without the living water which is Christ! Jesus said, "Whoever drinks the water I give him will never thirst again. Indeed, the water I give him will become in him a spring of water welling up to eternal life" (John 4:14 NIV).

We know from John chapter 1 that Jesus is the Word that became flesh and now dwells in us as believers. Therefore, as we water the garden of our soul, we must water it with the Word. This not only implies God's presence through His Spirit but also with His Word—the Holy Scriptures. We must feed on His Word, which is living and active, daily allowing it to become inculcated in our heart and mind.

When speaking of God's Word, there are different forms, or manifestations, that it takes. The first is the Word, *Logos*. This is the Greek word meaning "principle of divine reason and creative order," identified in the Gospel of John with the Second Person of the Trinity incarnate in Jesus Christ. Next is the Greek word *Rhema*. Here, the meaning is "action of utterance," God's Word spoken to us. It is that which inspires, reveals, and illuminates. Then there's the Greek word *Zoe*, meaning literally "life," living in us. This is what Jesus referred to in John 10:10, "I have come that they may have life, and have it abundantly."

God's Word dwelling in us, living in us—what a concept! Without it, we are spiritually dead, just as a farmer's crops are dead without water. And just as the farmer must be sedulous to water his crops daily, so also our watering with the Word ought to be a daily process. Not in some obligatory manner with a sense of routine but, rather, we should water our soul with the nourishment from God, with joyful and expectant hearts full of praise and thanksgiving.

Now, I am not a morning type of reader. That is to say, it's all I can do to get out of bed at 5:00 a.m. and get going to work on time most days. But whether someone is a morning person or a night owl, the important thing is to make time every day for taking in the life-giving water and nourishment of God's Word. We must make it a high priority. I love what Stephen Covey says about priorities: "The key is not to prioritize what's on your schedule, but to schedule your priorities" (*The 7 Habits of Highly Effective People*). Knowing and planning in advance what's most important and then ensuring there is time set aside, and guarded jealously, for that priority each day—that is how we can guarantee living daily in the Word.

Meditating on God's Word is what I am really referring to, not just simply reading verse after verse and then checking it off the list as a priority accomplished. Just as it says in Psalm 1:2–3,

> But his delight is in the law [Word] of the Lord; and in His Word does he meditate day and night. And he shall be like a tree planted by the rivers of water, that brings forth his fruit in his season; his leaf also shall not wither; and whatsoever he does shall prosper.

I have always been deeply impacted by how Satan knows the Scriptures also. Otherwise, he wouldn't have been able to quote verses from Psalm 91 while tempting our Savior in the wilderness. Knowing and quoting Bible verses is not feeding on God's Word. Anyone can learn to memorize something and then use it as a weapon or a manipulative tool for achieving their own selfish desires or agenda. This is one way the church has failed over the years in certain circles. At times, Christians have thrown around Bible verses as little darts aimed at hurting or imposing judgment, certainly not ubiquitously, but nonetheless, all too often. That's why we as Christians are often referred to as "Bible thumpers" by those who are nonbelievers. This certainly must break our Heavenly Father's heart!

The psalmist David writes in Psalm 19:7–11:

> The Word of the LORD is perfect, refreshing the soul. The statutes of the LORD are trustworthy, making wise the simple. The precepts of the LORD are right, giving joy to the heart. The commands of the LORD are radiant, giving light to the eyes. The fear of the LORD is pure, enduring forever. The decrees of the LORD are firm, and all of them are righteous. They are more precious than gold, than much pure gold; they are sweeter than honey, than honey from the honeycomb. By them your servant is warned; in keeping them there is great reward.

There is powerful peace and assurance in taking God at His Word. Too often we fail to remember that the standard God holds us to as His people is commensurate with the standard He expects from us. By that I mean, just as God expects us to keep our word when we make a promise to Him, so also He wants us to expect, more so, count on Him keeping His promises. Malachi 3:10 is proof of this postulation:

> "Bring the whole tithe into the storehouse, that there may be food in my house. Test me in this," says the LORD Almighty, "and see if I will not throw open the floodgates of heaven and pour out so much blessing that there will not be room enough to store it."

Another promise worth "holding" God to is found in Philippians 1:6: "Being confident of this, that He who began a good work in you will carry it on to completion until the day of Christ Jesus." We must always remember, God is not done with us yet, and He won't be until we get to heaven where Jesus awaits our homecoming. Also, I have found great strength and comfort in praying the following passage of Scripture back to God during times of uncertainty. "So it is with my word that goes out from my mouth: It will not return to me empty or void, but will accomplish what I desire and achieve the purpose for which I sent it" (Isaiah 55:11).

God's Word is a solid foundation we can build our life upon. Jesus is the Word, living and active in and around us, even when we can't see it. Still, He is working behind the scenes, as in the same way a theatrical master carpenter would work behind the scenes, preparing the set for the next act. God does not get tired; He never needs to stop and take a break. He is constantly and sedulously working, creating a new scene for the next act in our performance called life.

There's a creative aspect to the Word of God, which is what the word *Zoe* really means, creating life. It's the truth of Proverbs 18:21, which reminds us that the power of life and death is in the spoken word—our spoken word, not just God's spoken word. That's some creative force for sure that people can wield, either as a life-creating catalyst or as a destructive weapon of death. We must be very careful to ensure we are faithful stewards of this entrusted power the LORD has given us as mortal beings.

Therefore, let's read and study the Word of God with the intent to understand and grow closer to God, not to stand on higher ground than someone else or stock up with ammunition to use against them. We should always pray that the LORD will reveal His Word to us in a life-giving, life-changing way. Then we can live each day as humble, healthy spiritual "gardens" full of vital nutrients that can be shared with those along our journey. It's as we reflect, not deflect, God's Word that people who don't know Him yet will be drawn into a saving knowledge of Jesus Christ, the Messiah. They will see the words of Christ spoken through us in how we live, not just in what we say. This is the contagious attraction, drawing others to Christ, that we must exude to cultivate a fertile soil, seeded with praise and flowing with living wells of life-giving water.

# CHAPTER 6

# Protecting with Prayer

A meticulous farmer or gardener would certainly never forget to take some preventive measure to protect what they're growing. Whether it's an organic pesticide or some natural type of protective screening, what's most important to them is that the forthcoming harvest is safe and secure. It is the same with the garden of our soul. We are growing something beautiful and enduring, provided we protect that which God is doing with prayer. I am referring to a consistently devoted type of prayer. It's easy to pray for a few days or maybe a couple of weeks with a methodical and sedulous approach—a commitment with the best of intentions. But then life happens. The tax returns reveal a burdensome liability you weren't expecting. The kids come down with the latest sickness going around at school. Or perhaps it's your job that is consuming entirely too much of your time lately. Regardless of the excuse or justified reason, your "New Year's resolution" suddenly dissipates like the morning dew after a nighttime deluge.

Now you're left wondering why those challenges and obstacles are draining all your energy and hope. The reason is easy to detect but often hard to admit. Unbeknownst, you've put God on the back shelf of your life. God is understanding, of course, but relentlessly jealous. He beckons to you through the strangest of ways sometimes just to get your attention and focus back on Him. The key is to know how to recognize those signs of pining from the LORD. Remember, He wants to be the lover of your soul.

This is where accountability within the safety of community and family is essential. Just as the farmer has a spouse and most likely a banker who are both going to be watching to ensure he is doing everything necessary to protect the crop, so also God is going to go to extreme measures to pursue us and draw us onto Himself. It's best to make that process as painless as possible. What I mean is don't wait until the LORD must allow (not cause) some serious adversity to get your attention with an alarming wake-up call. Be proactive and make sure you have at least a couple of trusted friends or family members you can count on to ask you regularly how your prayer life is. It is quite the pernicious strategy of the enemy, Satan, to lull us into a false sense of security, making us believe that somehow we're immune to this danger of a stagnant prayer life all because we've been a Christian for so many years. Wrong!

Don't be fooled. Take well-formulated steps to plan out your offensive attack. That's right, we need to stop being defensive Christians. Being defensive as a driver is the correct approach, but not as a prayer warrior, when we are battling against "principalities, powers, and rulers of this dark world." We must remember, Satan comes to steal, kill, and destroy. It's not enough for him to merely give you a bad day; he wants you to have a bad life! Take the offensive posture and get on your knees to fight with the greatest weapon you could ever have—prayer!

The Bible says in 2 Corinthians 10:3–5,

> For though we walk in the flesh, we do not war according to the flesh. For the weapons of our warfare are not carnal but mighty in God for pulling down strongholds, casting down arguments and every high thing that exalts itself against the knowledge of God, bringing every thought into captivity to the obedience of Christ.

Prayer is our main weapon to war against all that would try to steal our joy, peace, and hope in Christ. Prayer, powerful travailing prayer, is always the best way to know what God wants to do in your life and through you.

The Bible is another great weapon, as mentioned in the previous chapter. And when you combine both prayer and the Word together, look out, you'll be able to say with confidence that only comes from God, "No weapon formed against me will prosper." The following are some proactive measures we can all take as soldiers in the battle of our soul:

*Go away regularly to a designated place of prayer, a prayer and worship center, or perhaps a spiritual retreat center.* Pick one day each week at least—preferably more, if possible—to go to a special location, even if it's just your church or prayer closet at home. However, since churches aren't usually open 24/7, you could seek out a local community center or prayer room that's available in the evenings or weekends. The point is to be deliberate to set aside a specific time and a specific place to pray. This, of course, is in addition to what 1 Thessalonians 5:17 instructs us to do: "Pray continually." Again, what Stephen Covey said applies here also with prayer, "The key is not to prioritize what's on your schedule, but to schedule your priorities."

*Ask a trusted friend to check on you regularly and ask some tough personal questions about where you are spiritually.* Give them permission to speak into your life, but first make sure they are worthy of that trust and influence. All too often, we pick the person who will say what we want to hear. This battle is too important to choose someone who will merely pander to your personal predilections or be afraid of offending you. Instead, choose someone you know who has lived and especially walked with the LORD long enough to provide wise and godly counsel. That's the kind of advice we all need. "Plans fail for lack of counsel, but with many advisers they succeed" (Proverbs 15:22 NIV).

Listen to worship songs on the radio while driving and at home. Fill your soul with life-giving songs of praise to God. Be mindful and protective of what you watch on television, at the movies, or on your computer and phone. Remember the old saying, "Garbage in, garbage out." Fill up with Scripture verses from audio CDs. Surround yourself with artwork that prompts you to think on the things of God. Music and art can be powerful stimuli to promote spiritual renewal.

Speaking of prayer centers earlier, in my thirties, my favorite place to be when I wasn't with my son was the World Prayer Center in Colorado Springs. I would love to go there in the evening or whenever I could. They had a regular prayer and worship time in the main sanctuary every Friday. One Friday I was driving back from Denver, and I sensed the Holy Spirit tell me to stop for that noon service. Of course, being all too glad to obey, I stopped and went inside to pray. While I was standing in a corner praying, an elderly woman I had never met nor seen before came walking up to me and said, "What the LORD is saying about you is, He sees you as a David, as a man after His own heart."

Now, the reason this was so incredibly moving to me and made me immediately drop to my knees was because just prior to her wonderful interruption, I had just been praying, "LORD, I want desperately for you to make me a man after your own heart!" That was, and remains, one of the most spiritually profound moments of my life. After she finished "reading my spiritual mail," telling me things that were impossible for her to know otherwise, she simply walked away. Her obedience to the LORD provided confirmation in my soul that has sustained me in some of life's darker moments and equipped me for battle many times since. That happened all because of earnest, surrendered prayer.

Now, there are several different types of prayer, such as intercessory, strategic, transformative, listening, identification, repentant, healing, soaking, and meditating. And different times call for different types of prayer implemented. It's important to ask the LORD to show you which is the appropriate kind of prayer needed in every situation you face and at each season of your journey. These are some inspiring famous quotes concerning prayer that might help us understand what's called for when:

- "Prayer is essentially a partnership of the redeemed child of God working hand in hand with God toward the realization of His redemptive purposes on earth" (Jack Hayford).

- "Prayer enlarges the heart until it is capable of containing God's gift of Himself. Prayer is putting oneself in the hands of God and listening to His voice in the depth of our hearts" (Mother Teresa).
- "The continuance of your longing is the continuance of your prayer" (St. Augustine).
- "To fall in love with God is the greatest romance; to seek Him, the greatest adventure; to find Him, the greatest human achievement" (St. Augustine).
- Matthew 26 describes Jesus praying in the garden prior to His crucifixion, "'Father, if You are willing, remove this cup from me. Nevertheless, not my will, but Yours, be done.' And there appeared to Him an angel from heaven, strengthening Him."

It is in those dark and desperate moments when we feel as if all hope is lost that a simple prayer, a cry for help to the LORD, can turn everything around. Our perspective, which was, just moments earlier, bleak and dismal now seems as if light is shining through. The light that can only come from the Father of heavenly lights, which exposes the deepest crevasses in our soul, where darkness and despair had made their uninvited home. Then, as is always the case, the light dispels the darkness, evicting it from our soul, bringing a glimpse of hope back into focus. This turning point can only be precipitated by heartfelt prayer, whether it's your own or perhaps some-one interceding on your behalf. Scripture says, "His Spirit intercedes for us with groanings that words cannot even express" (Romans 8:26).

It is a common symptom of the human con-dition to allow a thing to become the idol that we worship. This thing can be anything from a robust bank account, a relationship like marriage, the min-istry we know God called us to, or even a place we refuse to consider leaving, no matter who sent us there in the first place. All these things might be on the surface very noble, good, and even God's will. But we become so stuck in the familiar and what's comfortable that we inadvertently trade perfect peace and freedom for safety. Yet in the end, the only thing we are safe from is experiencing true joy and con-tentment in Christ. This is the tragic grand illusion. Benjamin Franklin once said, "Those who would give up essential Liberty to purchase a little tempo-rary Safety deserve neither Liberty nor Safety."

This is why it's so very prudent to remind our-selves to pray for what's next in our journey with openness and excitement. We must stop thinking we've arrived and simply put life on "cruise con-trol"—when life truly surrendered to God requires capitulating all control to Him, and embracing change if God desires. Life in Jesus Christ was never supposed to be predictable, static, nor easy.

But prayer—consistent, intimate prayer where we lay our heart wide open before the LORD—is the only way to maintain perfect peace (shalom, shalom) in the midst of whatever is next. As we take this vulnerable and sometimes scary step into the unknown, trusting only in God, we will discover revelations from His Spirit, in His timing, that serve as stepping-stones, allowing us to walk across the water we once saw as impossible. But just as Peter began to sink once he took his eyes off Jesus, so also we must keep our face fixed on His if we are ever to see the miraculous occur. It's how we realize God's purpose and plan for us fulfilled in our lifetime!

I've heard it said, attitude is everything. And while I know it's not everything, it is immeasurably significant to how we face what's next. Whether what's next is a new job, a relocation to a new home, or perhaps the ending of a bittersweet friendship, taking that journey with the LORD, our Comforter and Rock, with the right attitude will see us through to the other side where peace and understanding await. Prayer is the vessel that gets us to the other shore across the waters of change.

Remember, as you pray, don't be so concerned about what you say but rather practice listening, being still before God, and let Him speak to you. This is where the art of meditation can really help. In our fast-paced society, where we want everything right now and patience is a dying virtue (especially with me), the concept of sitting still before God with no distractions and waiting for Him to speak is very hard to comprehend for some. It is a prevalent misconception that to pray effectively, we must know all the right words to say; somehow the holier we sound and the faster we say it, the more God hears us. Nothing could be farther from the truth.

What God wants more than anything, I believe, is our life surrendered and our heart open to Him. It is when we admit who we really are before Him, with transparent and humble "groans," that His heart is moved and then moves on our behalf. Don't be afraid to remind God, as if He needed reminding, what He has promised in His Word. One such promise might be what James 4:8 says, "Draw near to God and He will draw near to you."

One of my favorite stories in the Old Testament is about King Hezekiah. Second Kings 20 records the brief second prayer of Hezekiah: "Remember now, O LORD, I beseech thee, how I have walked before thee in truth and with a whole heart and have done what is good in thy sight." Scripture tells us it was this prayer that literally changed God's mind. What a concept to consider! That prayer could actually cause God to decide not to do something He was planning to do. Earlier in this passage from 2 Kings, we learn that God had sent the prophet Isaiah to inform a very ill Hezekiah to "get his affairs in order, for he would surely die, very soon." Now, we must understand this was most definitely not a test or some kind of bluff. God sincerely meant what He said through the prophet.

But then the remarkable happened. Hezekiah dared to remind God of some very important facts. We find in the book of Deuteronomy chapter 4 that

God had made certain promises many years earlier to the children of Israel, stating,

> So you shall keep my statutes and my commandments which I am giving you today, that it may go well with you and your children after you, and that you may prolong your days on the land which the LORD your God is giving you for all time.

Then after reciting this promise, Hezekiah took it a step further. He prayed the heartfelt prayer mentioned earlier, reminding God of how faithful and obedient he had been before the LORD all his life.

Some might go as far as to say that was arrogant and presumptuous on Hezekiah's part. I would strongly disagree. I would suggest it was Hezekiah simply being real and transparent before God. And, in turn, that sincerity paid off for sure. We find that after Hezekiah finished praying, and as Isaiah was walking away, something amazing took place. God said to Isaiah,

> Go back and tell Hezekiah, the leader of my people, "This is what the LORD, the God of your father David, says: I have heard your prayer and seen your tears; I will heal you. On the third day

from now you will go up to the temple of the LORD. I will add fifteen years to your life."

This is a compelling picture for us to show how important and effective prayer can be. It is an excellent example of James 5:16, "The prayer of a righteous man (or woman) is powerful and effective." Yet it was especially effective because of Hezekiah's palpable authenticity and anguish, his understanding of God's promises and sovereign protection, and due to his faithful and obedient walk with the LORD, which can only come from a place of true intimacy. In the end, it resulted in a harvest of joy from a prolonged life!

# CHAPTER 7

# Harvest of Joy

Nothing evokes the feelings of life on a farm like harvesttime. The cool, crisp autumn air filled with hope and the "bovine blessing" dispelling all the struggles of summer—the torrential storms, the toiling labor, and back-breaking hours in incessant heat. Now that refreshing fall breeze reminds you that those "dog days" are past. Winter lies ahead and, with it, the hope of peace. But first, it's time to bring forth the fruits of your labor.

So you've done all the prerequisites to prepare for harvest. You've plowed the soil of your soul to break up that fallow ground. You've extracted all those pernicious weeds of your past sins and bad habits. You've planted healthy, fruitful seeds of praise and gratitude, and even fertilized with the beautiful nutrients of friendship. You were even diligent to water every day with the holy water of God's Word and protect that which God had birthed in you with fervent prayer. And now it's time to reap what you've sown. But there's a problem: the harvest isn't quite what you expected.

Sure, it may be somewhat fruitful and still good. It may even be beneficial for others, but it's not as plentiful or vibrant as you had hoped. You're disappointed and perhaps discouraged. So like any good farmer worth his salt, you begin to examine the crop your heart and soul just yielded, and you realize you left out one vital ingredient—the "Sonshine of surrender." Now, before you start to think there's a misspelled word, allow me to explain. The sunshine I am referring to can only come from the Son of God, Jesus. He alone provides the life-giving radiance that makes your soul blessed abundantly and your heart filled with effervescent joy. As the old hymn says, "Joy unspeakable and full of glory."

But why do we miss out on that essential blessing sometimes? Most likely, it's because we forget the latter part of the ingredient—surrender. We make the all-too-common mistake of trying to do it all on our own, in our own strength and humanity. I am not implying we didn't do the work. In fact, that's just the problem; it was work. When we surrender everything we have, everything we are to God and ask Him to take over with complete control, and do the "heavy lifting," we find the entire process becomes joyful, not burdensome. It is imperative, though, that we recognize the truth of John 15:5, where Jesus said, "I am the vine; you are the branches. If you remain in me and I in you, you will bear much fruit; apart from me you can do nothing."

What do I mean, you ask? Well, I would compare it to when we were first courting our spouse. The man would open the door without having to be asked and bring flowers without even needing a reminder. The lady would shower her future betrothed with compliments and affection without even thinking about it. Then, after the honeymoon was long over, those same things became work. So it is with our journey of faith. When we're first saved, everything comes so easily and seems so natural. The feeding on God's Word and spending quality time in prayer and worship is a joy and delight.

Then, after the spiritual honeymoon is over, we find it takes all our conscious attention and effort to keep those habits going. Perhaps the real issue is we need to stop seeing the feeding on and studying of Scripture, as well as prayer and worship, as a habit. In the flesh (our human nature), that's all it can be. But, in the spirit, a heart and soul completely surrendered to God, it couldn't be farther from work. Once again, it becomes a joyful expression of love, gratitude, and devotion to our Savior. After all, Scripture tells us that Christ is to be "the lover of our soul." He is our magnificent obsession! In Genesis 15:1, God told Abraham, "I am your exceedingly great reward." When was the last time we thanked God for being those same attributes to us?

Surrendering ourselves to the Almighty, in a similar way to when we surrender ourselves to our spouse upon matrimony, is how we discover that true joy and intimacy. They say reality is 90 percent perception. There is some truth to that. Perhaps all it takes is an ongoing reminder each day to purposefully have the correct perception. The perception that says I am a child of the Most High God. I am beloved by my Creator, fearfully and wonderfully made by Him. I am endowed with every spiritual blessing I need. I am strong in the LORD and in the power of His might! I am an overcomer in Christ, set apart (sanctified) to be a royal priesthood offering spiritual sacrifices of praise and worship to the one true Living God.

Also, I believe with true surrender, there is an essential piece of how we perceive our daily cares. John Denver had a song in the '70s called "Sweet Surrender." It was one of my father's favorite songs. Part of the song goes like this:

> There's nothin' behind me and
> nothin' that ties me to
> something that might have
> been true yesterday.
> Tomorrow is open, right now
> it seems to be more than
> enough to just be here today,
> and I don't know

What the future is holdin' in store.
I don't know where I'm goin' I'm
not sure where I've been.
There's a spirit that guides me, a
light that shines for me.
My life is worth the livin', I don't
need to see the end.

Sweet, sweet surrender, live, live
without care…

I remember thinking when I first heard the song many years ago as a kid that those last words "live without care" sounded a little hippie-ish. But now, as a grown man five decades later, I really believe it's the same as what Peter was referring to in 1 Peter 5:7: "Casting all your cares upon Him, for He careth for you." God clearly wants us to lay all our cares, concerns, and burdens on Him. It is His divine will that we live childlike lives full of faith in our Father, free from worry and strife. After all, Jesus did say, "Truly, I tell you, unless you change and become like little children, you will never enter the kingdom of heaven" (Matthew 18:3 NIV). Certainly, a daunting task for us all as adults who have already succumbed to the sobering realities of life with all its adversity, pain, and stressful obligations.

How do we then make the transformation and cross the mile-wide chasm back to the simpler life of a child? While I do understand, and even adhere to, Thoreau's reasoning for his exhortation to live a simpler life, I believe what the LORD Jesus was referring to in that verse from Matthew was living a life with the innocent, childlike mindset and outlook on life. This, of course, is only achievable when we allow the Holy Spirit to do His sanctifying work each day in our heart and mind. As David wrote in Psalm 51:10, "Create in me a pure heart, O God; and renew a steadfast spirit within me."

My dear grandmother Joanna loved to garden. I believe it was her favorite pastime, perhaps besides telling me stories of how she grew up in the early 1900s on a farm in the Missouri Ozarks. She found such joy in planning what she would plant next, then carefully tending to the seedlings with sedulous watering and care and eventually bringing forth the bountiful harvest of vegetables, which she then would prepare for her large family in the form of nourishing sustenance. Although she was in her seventies and eighties at those endearing times I remember so fondly spent with her in the garden, she always had a youthful ebullience that was infectious. It was truly reminiscent of how a child would play with excitement and anticipation.

Another wonderful picture of this childlike innocence and faith are two games I used to play with my dad when I was little and, likewise, my son, who is now a father himself, used to enjoy with me. When my son was just a couple years old, he would stand on top of a table and jump into my arms. The other game he loved to play was to stand in my hand (yes, one hand). It took great balance on his part and some strength on mine. But most of all, like the first game, it took incredible trust on my son's part.

When was the last time we took that leap of faith and sweet surrender into our loving Heavenly Father's arms? I am convinced that the longer I live, nothing will help us live in the moment and experience the harvest of joy in our lives more than simply the sweet surrender of standing in God's hand and trusting Him to hold us firm and strong!

That is the life God wants each of us to live.

# EFFECTIVE PRAYERS FOR A VICTORIOUS LIFE

# Attitude Prayer

Father God,

I thank You for who You are, for the gift of eternal life through Your Son, Jesus Christ, and for the faithful ministry and presence of Your Holy Spirit. Thank You, LORD, for every blessing of life! LORD, please forgive me for the sin of pride, arrogance, and high-mindedness. Forgive me for harboring critical, judgmental, and condescending thoughts and attitudes that prevent me from sharing in the victory of what You are doing in the world. Keep me, O LORD, from being like Jonah and not rejoicing in the salvation of others. Forgive me for believing the lie that You love some more than others. God, help me to see everyone through Your eyes and love them like You do with Your heart of compassion, mercy, and grace. I choose to obey You, God, and surrender to Your perfect will. LORD, help me to embrace and maintain the right attitude of heart every day—to realize that obedience and surrender are not good enough without an attitude of love, joy, peace, generosity, and humility towards humanity.

I thank You that Your Word judges my thoughts and attitudes. Forgive me for seeing other people as the enemy instead of remembering there is only one real enemy—the one You defeated on the Cross and through an empty tomb! LORD, keep me from all captious and self-serving motives and attitudes. Help me take every thought captive and make it obedient unto Christ. Create in me a pure heart, O God, and cultivate a spirit of humility and constant worship unto You!

Make me ever mindful that to truly be a man after Your own heart means I must embrace others with Your heart of unconditional love and acceptance. Help me to remember it is not enough to merely believe in You, God, but that I must also believe You and every word You have spoken. I choose to acknowledge You, God, in all my ways! Remove from within me all doubt, unholy fear, and trepidation— and replace it with holy reverence and awe unto You! I want to walk in the fear of the LORD all of my days. May I always run into Your open arms, Heavenly Father. Cause strong abiding faith to grow within my life—to believe You, LORD, for the miraculous.

Thank You, Father, for loving me with an everlasting love and merciful compassion. Work full forgiveness in me towards others and myself, for I know You desire mercy more than sacrifice. May I always remember that Your forgiveness is related to how I forgive others. Instill within me a compassionate forbearance towards everyone I come in contact with.

Make me a blessing to all within my sphere of influence, I pray. Help me receive and embrace correction and discipline, as well as the Holy Spirit's conviction, as the life-giving blessing You intend for it to be. Please, Lord, grant me true and quick repentance that leads to a changed heart and mind. Give me the wisdom and discernment to recognize when the heart of any problem is actually a problem of the heart. Break up the fallow ground in my heart and make it soft and tender to receive the Seed of Truth that You desire to grow within me. Help me understand that prayer is the vessel that carries me safely to the other shore, across the waters of trial and transformation. I commit to being a person of sedulous prayer and partnering with You, God, to see Your kingdom come and Your will accomplished here on earth! In the mighty name of Jesus, amen.

## Breakthrough Prayer

On the authority of Jesus's name, I declare every word curse or negative confession ever spoken against me is broken here and now and therefore has no power or influence in my life. I thank You, God, that no weapon formed against me will prosper. I hereby renounce, cancel, and bind any unholy soul ties or alliances away from my life in the powerful name of Jesus. I confess and repent of any sin of idolatry or rebellion. I receive Your forgiveness and mercy, LORD. Thank You! And I choose to come into full covenant agreement with You, LORD God, concerning all Your laws, commands, and will for my life! Please, God, set me free from any and all generational curses or iniquities. I thank You, God, that the truth of who You are, and who I am in Christ, a new creation, sets me free indeed. I declare I am free from the bondage of sin. I am free to live the victorious life You have created me to live! I thank You that You have chosen me and set me apart to be a royal, holy priesthood offering spiritual sacrifices of worship unto the LORD Most High. I embrace the truth and reality that I have been engrafted into the seed of Abraham through Christ Jesus. Therefore, I receive, as a co-heir with Christ, the full blessing, freedom, and favor of God—in the mighty name of Jesus, amen.

## Sanctifying Prayer

LORD God, please make me into a vessel of honor in Your house. I want to be sanctified and useful for You, Master, prepared for every good work. Help me to flee all youthful lusts and to pursue righteousness, faith, love, and peace with those who call on You, LORD, out of a pure heart. Empower me to avoid all foolish disputes, for I know they generate strife. Help me to always remember that a servant of the LORD must not quarrel but instead be gentle to all, patient, able to teach. Teach me humility, Holy

Spirit, so I may be used by You, speaking the truth in love, to correct those who have been taken captive by the enemy.

Heavenly Father, I thank You that I am set apart by Your sovereign will and that You are refining me daily to be more like Jesus. Fill me with all the fruit of the Spirit, I pray. Help me grow in love, joy, peace, patience, kindness, goodness, faithfulness, gentleness, and self-control. I choose to surrender every area of my life to Your sanctifying work and transformative power and grace. I submit to Your kingdom authority, LORD, and to Your righteous rule and reign in my heart, soul, and entire life. I also choose to submit to the earthly authorities You have established over me for my protection and ultimate good. Please, God, place the right people in my life whom I can be accountable to. As iron sharpens iron, I pray You would use them to sharpen me. Sanctify me by the truth, O LORD, Your Word is truth! In Your most holy name I pray, amen.

## Protection Prayer

Living God, I thank You for the faithful protection in my life You have provided. Thank You for the promise in Your Word that as I acknowledge Your name, You will continue to protect me and rescue me—because I love You with all my heart! Please watch over me and keep me from all harm. I pray for health and safety as I continue to put my trust in You alone, for You are my refuge and mighty fortress.

Your faithfulness is my shield and rampart! I thank You that You have commanded Your angels concerning me to guard me in all my ways. Help me feed on Your Word, for it is a light unto my path, which will keep me from being detoured from Your will. I ask for Your almighty protection over the calling, talents, and treasures You have placed in my life. In the mighty name of Jesus I pray, amen.

## Healing Prayer

Jesus, I thank You that it's by Your wounds, which You bore on the Cross, that I am healed. I acknowledge that You are the Almighty Healer, the Great Physician. I also realize that while You are able to heal any and all sickness and disease, it may not always be Your will to do so here on earth. I thank You that, as a child of God, I will for sure receive full healing and complete restoration in Heaven. I pray that You will give me the grace and strength to endure, and the faith to believe. I do trust You, LORD, for healing and protection. I surrender this infirmity to You, laying it at the foot of the Cross. Help me, O LORD, to trust You more and to understand Your perfect will for my life. Help me to always be mindful of the needs of others, especially those oppressed and less fortunate. I pray that You will give me the strength, even in the midst of my own struggles, to be a blessing to those within my sphere of influence. Help me remember, as Your Word promises:

to loose the chains of injustice
and untie the cords of the yoke,
to set the oppressed free
and break every yoke,
to share food with the hungry
and to provide the poor wanderer
    with shelter,
to clothe the naked,
and not to turn away from my
    own flesh and blood.
Then my light will break forth
    like the dawn,
and my healing will quickly appear.

Holy Spirit, I ask for Your divine anointing in every cell of my body and fiber of my being. Please heal me, O LORD, for You are my portion and my praise! I choose to worship You, Living God, in the midst of this trial, knowing You will be my strength and my song—my hope is in You. Help me keep my eyes fixed on You, my refuge and mighty fortress! I thank You for the promise and assurance that You hear my prayer. In the powerful name of Jesus I pray, amen.

## Repentant Prayer

LORD, I confess all of my sins and transgressions against You. I acknowledge that I am a sinner saved by Your grace only through faith in Jesus Christ. I want to live the victorious life I was created by You to live. Therefore, by the power of the Holy Spirit living in me, I repent of all my sinful disobedience and plead the precious blood of Jesus to wash away my iniquities. Cleanse me from all unrighteousness, I pray, O Lord. I choose to return to You as my first love. Help me to rend my heart with humble transparency, and to abandon all carnal desires. I receive and embrace Your faithful forgiveness and mercy. Empower me by Your grace to go from victory to victory, as an overcomer in Christ! I want You, Jesus, to be the Lord of my life in every area, no exceptions. Praise You, Father, that I have become the righteousness of God because of what Your Son, Jesus, did for me on the Cross. I thank You that I am a new creation in Christ—the old man has been crucified and is dead and buried. And the new man has been raised to new abundant life in Jesus Christ. It's in His Holy name that I pray, amen.

## Discernment Prayer

Lord, I need Your guidance and direction in my life always. Please help me as I navigate this decision and crossroad I am facing. Give me the wisdom and discernment I need. Help me to hear Your voice clearly as I lean into Your presence and spend time feeding on Your Word. Your will for my life is perfect and just, I know that full well. I ask that You, O God, would make my path straight as I trust in You with all my heart. Help me not to lean on my own understanding, but instead, I choose to acknowledge

You, LORD, in all my ways. I know You have an awesome plan for my life, a plan to prosper me and give me hope and a future. Thank You, God! Please surround me with faithful people who know You and walk in constant communion with You so they might walk alongside me through this journey and provide insight, discernment, and confirmation by the power of Your Holy Spirit. Increase the faith within me so I can step out boldly, testing the waters of change, as You lead and guide me by Your sovereign hand. I put my hope and trust in You alone, Living God. For it is in You that I live and move and have my being! I thank You, LORD, and praise You in advance for the direction and peace I know You will provide. In the mighty name of Jesus, amen.

## Thankful Prayer

God, I thank You for every good and perfect gift that comes from Your hand! You have blessed me abundantly in so many ways, I could never recount them all. Thank You, Father, for Your faithfulness, loving-kindness, forgiveness, mercy, and grace. I praise You for Your generosity, healing, protection, provision, anointing, and favor in my life. I recognize everything I am and have comes from You. It all belongs to You, LORD. Help me be a faithful steward with a grateful heart. I choose to worship You in my giving and serving. Help me reflect Your lavish generosity and love in how I bless others with the talents, time, and treasures You have entrusted me with.

Make me always mindful to show appreciation and gratitude without reservation—both to You and to others. You are worthy and deserving of all the praise, honor, glory, and thanks now and forevermore! In the wonderful name of Jesus, I pray, amen.

## Intercessory Prayer

Almighty God, I stand in the gap before You on behalf of __________. Please do a miracle in their life today. A miracle of healing, deliverance, provision, or whatever they need. You alone know what is best for them, and I thank You that You are the answer to their deepest need. LORD, I pray that __________ will turn to You and trust in You alone. Remove any obstacles and distractions from their life that would prevent them from hearing Your voice and knowing Your perfect will. I pray that You, O God, would bind any foul, unclean spirit that would come against them and the plan You have for their life. Please, God, break off every negative confession or generational curse away from __________. Help them embrace the truth of who they have been created to be in Christ Jesus. My prayer is that __________ would receive everything You want to impart in their life. I pray a strong passion would burn inside their heart to know You intimately. Please reveal Yourself to them in a powerful life-changing way. Give them a hunger and thirst for Your life-giving Word. Bless them, LORD, richly and abundantly. Consume them with Your holy presence and relentless love. Fill them with Your perfect peace

that passes all understanding. I thank You, God, that
___________ has been given a spirit of power, of love,
and of a sound mind, and that Your perfect love is
casting out all worldly fear from their life! I pray this
all in the mighty name of Jesus, amen.

## Transitional (Waiting) Prayer

Father, I confess that waiting is not always an
easy thing to do. But I know You are growing me
into a person of deep abiding faith, and that the cru-
cible of growth takes time. Help me, O LORD, to be
patient and wait on You. I thank You for the promises
of Your Word that are ever faithful and true, and that
Your Word will not return empty or void but will
accomplish what You desire. Thank You, God, that
as I wait on You during this time of transition, You
will renew my strength. Help me be still before You,
my Rock and Mighty Fortress. In Your shelter, I find
hope and peace and protection. God, help me learn
contentment even in this "in-between" place. I thank
You, Holy Spirit, that You are here with me and will
guide me through this temporal place of transition.
Help me remember that through the eyes of eternity, this period of waiting is but a fleeting moment.
LORD, I acknowledge Your timing is always perfect!
I choose to keep my eyes fixed on You, O LORD, and
worship You in whatever season I am in. I love Your
presence, and I thank You that in Your presence is
perfect peace and fullness of joy forever! I pray this
all in the awesome and precious name of Jesus, amen.

## Intimacy Prayer

Living God, You alone are my magnificent obsession, my exceedingly great reward! You are my first love, the lover of my soul. My heart and soul long for You and for Your holy presence. There is no place I'd rather be than in Your living sanctuary. I thank You that You know me better than I know myself. For You search my heart and test me, to grow me into a person after Your own heart. Selah! Abba Father, I thank You for Your extravagant love and affection towards me. Thank You for drawing me unto Yourself. As I enter into the inner courts of Your presence, I will dance before You as You sing over me! You are my love song and my heart's desire. Please reveal Yourself more and more to me as I seek You with all my heart and soul. Thank You for the promises of Your Word. Strip away from me all the outer garments of pride and shame that would keep me from truly abiding in You and knowing You fully, even as I am fully known by You. I humble myself before You, God. My spirit cries out to worship You in the glory and splendor of Your holiness—I am undone by Your majesty and righteousness! I love You, LORD, with all my heart, soul, and strength. Thank You for Your relentless pursuit of my heart. I will pursue You all the days of my life, and I will dwell in the house of the LORD forever! In the most holy name of Jesus, I respond to You, LORD, with yes and amen!

# EPILOGUE

If the reader has found themselves motivated by this book to either connect with God for the first time or perhaps reconnect with God, then the following is my humble suggestion of next steps.

After praying the prayer of salvation (accepting Christ Jesus as your Savior and Lord) or praying the prayer of rededicating your life to Christ, find the right church to become involved with. Make sure to do ample research and confirm it is a Bible-based, Spirit-filled church. What do I mean by that? It should be a church that believes the Bible is the authoritative and inerrant Word of God, inspired by the Holy Spirit. Next, while it's not essential the church is charismatic necessarily, unless that is what resonates with you, it should be a church that believes and operates in the "gifts of the Spirit." Per Scripture, these include but are not limited to teaching, prophecy, encouraging, compassion, works of healing, leading, discernment, wisdom, knowledge, and faith. I would strongly encourage reading 1 Corinthians chapter 12 for further expository explanation. It is important to always remember, just as the Bible teaches, not everyone has the same gifts, but everyone has some gifts. We are all created with unique gifts and talents from God. It is vital that we discover those gifts and talents and use them for God's glory and others' benefit.

Another essential attribute to look for in a healthy, life-giving church is love. Is it a warm and welcoming environment, regardless of a person's stage in life, where a person can get connected easily and feel at home? To facilitate this happening, be sure to check what the small group infrastructure is like. The reason for this important statement is small groups within a church is where accountability and growth occur. Especially within a large church setting, healthy and diverse small groups are essential to promote a sense of belonging and community. Some churches call this by a different name, such as free-market cell groups, life groups, or home-church Bible studies, but the concept is the same and highly recommended. It is entirely too easy to hide out in a church, especially a large church.

And while one might still receive sound biblical teaching and a great worship experience, as soon as life throws a curveball with some unforeseen challenge or crisis, that's when having that strong small group of community, where intimacy and support have been cultivated, will pay dividends. Also, be sure the church has a strong and vital prayer ministry. And while hearing "Christ crucified and risen" being preached is certainly the most important thing, remember the letters the apostle Paul wrote to the early church are full of challenging and even controversial issues, admonishments, and guidelines that go beyond the main thing—Christ crucified and risen. Therefore, look for a church that is not scared or embarrassed to teach countercultural messages.

Whatever you do, pick a church where the truth is taught that the individual can study and understand Scripture by themselves with insight and revelation from the Holy Spirit, and they don't have to go through some mediator (such as the pastor) to communicate with God. The LORD has made very clear throughout His Word that everyone can have direct access to God through the complete redemptive work of Jesus Christ on the Cross and by His saving grace and forgiveness alone. Therefore, everyone, through faith, can pray to God directly; and through the indwelling of the Holy Spirit, which we all receive at salvation, obtain instruction, correction, comfort, understanding, and encouragement from God. And make sure every believer is welcome there at the LORD's table for Holy Communion.

So pray and ask the LORD to guide you, and He will be faithful to complete the great work He has begun. Live the life you were meant to live by God's grace and with His Spirit living in you—live abundantly and extraordinarily in Christ!

And enjoy the gardening journey.

# ABOUT THE AUTHOR

David Mahan is a graduate of ministry from Wagner Leadership Institute (a.k.a. Wagner University). He is married and is the father of one son and five grandchildren. Dave is also the founder of Ezekiel Prayer Ministries and calls Arizona home. His passion is prayer and worship, as well as American history. Dave loves to help others realize their full potential in God's calling for their lives.